York Travel C

WITH 2,3 & 5-DAY ITINERARIES

CW00508047

York Minster and the York Skyline, from Clifford's Tower. Photo: <u>John Morgan</u>

Welcome to our comprehensive guide to York and the surrounding areas of Yorkshire! Whether you're a history buff, foodie, or outdoor enthusiast, there's something for everyone in this vibrant city and its stunning countryside.

In this guide, we will take you on a journey through the best attractions, hidden gems, food and drink options, shopping spots, and family-friendly activities in York. We will also provide tips and advice on planning your trip, getting around, and staying safe.

From exploring the iconic York Minster and strolling through the historic Shambles to indulging in traditional Yorkshire cuisine and experiencing the city's bustling nightlife, we've got you covered. And if you're interested in exploring beyond the city limits, we've included suggestions for day trips and excursions to nearby national parks, coastal towns, and scenic drives.

So sit back, relax, and let us be your guide to the best that York and Yorkshire have to offer!

Contents

Introduction 3

   1.1 A Brief History of York...............................3

   1.2 Why Visit York? 4

Planning Your Trip 6

   2.1 Best Time to Visit 6

   2.2 Entry Requirements and Visas....................7

   2.3 Budgeting for Your Trip 8

Getting to York...11

   3.1 By Air...11

   3.2 By Train..12

   3.3 By Bus..14

   3.4 By Car 15

Accommodation 17

   4.1 Hotels 17

   4.2 Bed & Breakfasts 18

   4.3 Hostels 19

   4.4 Self-Catering and Apartments....................20

   4.5 Unique Stays..21

   4.6 Our Top Suggestions 22

Transportation in York 23

   5.1 Public Transport...23

   5.2 Taxis and Rideshares 23

   5.3 Biking 23

   5.4 Walking 24

York's Top Attractions..25

Hidden Gems and Lesser-Known Attractions.........27

Food and Drink 29

8.1 Traditional Yorkshire Cuisine 29

8.2 Local Pubs and Bars 29

8.3 Afternoon Tea 30

8.4 Fine Dining and Gourmet Experiences 31

8.5 Vegetarian and Vegan Options 32

8.6 International Cuisine 32

Shopping and Souvenirs...34

9.1 Independent Shops and Boutiques 34

9.2 York's Markets...34

9.3 Antique and Vintage Finds 35

9.4 Art Galleries and Craft Shops 35

9.5 Shopping Centres and High Street Brands 36

Day Trips and Excursions...38

10.1 North York Moors National Park 38

10.2 Yorkshire Dales...38

10.3 Castle Howard..38

10.4 Fountains Abbey and Studley Royal Water Garden 38

10.5 Whitby and the Yorkshire Coast.......................39

10.6 Harrogate and Ripon.......................................39

10.7 The City of Leeds 39

10.8 The Brontë Parsonage and Haworth..................39

Festivals and Events...40

11.1 York Festival of Ideas......................................40

11.2 York Food and Drink Festival...........................40

11.3 York Races..40

11.4 York Christmas Market.....................................40

11.5 York Literature Festival 40

11.6 JORVIK Viking Festival.....................................40

11.7 York Early Music Festival 41

Nightlife and Entertainment 42

12.1 Theatre and Performing Arts 42

12.2 Live Music Venues 42

12.3 Cinemas 42

12.4 Comedy Clubs 42

12.5 Dance Clubs and Bars 42

12.6 Ghost Walks and Haunted Experiences 42

Travel Tips and Safety 44

13.1 Health and Medical Services 44

13.2 Accessibility and Mobility 44

13.3 Banking and Currency 44

13.4 Tipping and Gratuities 44

13.5 Staying Connected: Wi-Fi and Mobile Services 44

13.6 Local Customs and Etiquette 44

13.7 Emergency Contacts and Services 45

13.8 Weather and Climate 45

13.9 Language Tips and Useful Phrases 45

13.10 Safety Tips for Solo and Female Travelers 45

Family-Friendly York 47

14.1 Kid-Friendly Attractions 47

14.2 Family Dining Options 47

14.3 Outdoor Activities and Parks 47

14.4 Child-Friendly Accommodation 48

14.5 Tips for Traveling with Children 48

Beyond York: Exploring Yorkshire 49

16.1 Historic Cities and Towns 49

16.2 Coastal Towns and Beaches 49

16.3 Scenic Drives and Outdoor Adventures 49

Three-Day Detailed York Itinerary 51

    Day 1..51

    Day 2..54

    Day 3..57

Two-Day York Itinerary 59

Four & Five-Day York and Yorkshire Coast Itinerary...............61

Thank You! 65

Introduction

Welcome to Discovering York: Your Essential Travel Guide to the Heart of Yorkshire! York is a captivating city that effortlessly blends history, culture, and modernity. From ancient Roman walls to medieval streets and contemporary galleries, York offers a unique and unforgettable experience for travelers of all ages and interests. This comprehensive guide will help you plan the perfect trip to explore this charming city, its rich heritage, and its lively atmosphere.

1.1 A Brief History of York

York has a long and storied past that dates back over 2,000 years. The city was founded by the Romans in 71 AD as Eboracum, a strategic outpost of their empire. Over the centuries, it transformed from a Roman fortress to a thriving Viking trading center called Jorvik, before eventually becoming the royal and ecclesiastical capital of Northern England.

Throughout its history, York has played an important role in England's political and religious landscape. It has been a seat of power for Roman emperors, Viking kings, and medieval archbishops. In the Middle Ages, the city's prosperity and strategic location led to the construction of its iconic city walls and the stunning York Minster, which remains one of the finest examples of Gothic architecture in Europe.

The industrial revolution brought new industries to York, such as chocolate manufacturing, which left a lasting mark on the city's culture and economy. Today, York is a vibrant, modern city that embraces its past while looking toward the future. The city's rich heritage is evident in its well-preserved architecture, historic sites, and fascinating museums. At the same time, York boasts a thriving arts scene, contemporary dining options, and a bustling nightlife that caters to visitors and residents alike.

Tourism plays a significant role in York's economy, with millions of visitors each year coming to explore its ancient streets and attractions. In recent years, the city has made substantial efforts to become more sustainable and eco-friendly, focusing on green initiatives and supporting local businesses.

As you explore York, you will be captivated by its charming atmosphere and the warm hospitality of its people. Whether you're interested in delving into the city's storied past, indulging in culinary delights, or simply enjoying a leisurely stroll along the picturesque city walls, York offers a diverse array of experiences that are sure to make your visit a memorable one.

1.2 Why Visit York?

York is a destination that effortlessly combines history, culture, and natural beauty, making it an ideal choice for travelers seeking a well-rounded and unforgettable experience. Here are some of the top reasons to visit York:

1. **Rich history:** York's 2,000-year-old history is visible at every turn, from its ancient Roman walls to the cobbled streets of the medieval city center. Visiting York is like taking a step back in time, offering countless opportunities to explore and learn about its fascinating past.
2. **Stunning architecture:** The city boasts a remarkable array of architectural styles, with the York Minster as its crowning jewel. This Gothic masterpiece is one of the largest and most impressive cathedrals in Northern Europe, drawing visitors from around the world.
3. **Charming atmosphere:** York's narrow, winding streets, and historic buildings create an enchanting and atmospheric setting that is perfect for leisurely strolls and exploration.
4. **World-class museums: With** a wealth of museums covering everything from Viking history to railways and chocolate, York has something for every interest.
5. **Excellent dining options:** York's vibrant food scene offers a diverse range of culinary experiences, from traditional Yorkshire fare to international cuisine, fine dining, and award-winning restaurants.

6. **Shopping and markets:** York is a shopper's paradise, with a mix of independent boutiques, high street brands, and lively markets offering local produce and crafts.
7. **Natural beauty**: York is surrounded by stunning landscapes, including the North York Moors National Park, the Yorkshire Dales, and the picturesque Yorkshire coast. These natural wonders provide the perfect backdrop for a variety of outdoor activities such as hiking, cycling, and wildlife watching.
8. **Festivals and events:** Throughout the year, York hosts a number of lively festivals and events celebrating its culture, history, and local talent. From the JORVIK Viking Festival to the York Food and Drink Festival, there is always something happening to entertain and inspire visitors.
9. **Day trips and excursions:** York's central location in Northern England makes it an ideal base for exploring the surrounding regions. Excursions to nearby attractions like Castle Howard, Fountains Abbey, and the Brontë Parsonage offer unique opportunities to further discover the history and beauty of Yorkshire.
10. **Friendly and welcoming locals:** York's residents are known for their warmth and hospitality, making visitors feel at home from the moment they arrive. This welcoming atmosphere, combined with the city's charm and countless attractions, ensures that a visit to York is a truly unforgettable experience.

Whether you're a history buff, a food lover, a nature enthusiast, or simply someone looking for a charming city break, York has something to offer everyone. This vibrant and historic city will captivate your senses and leave you with lasting memories of your time spent exploring its ancient streets and hidden gems.

Planning Your Trip

2.1 Best Time to Visit

Deciding when to visit York largely depends on your personal preferences and interests, as the city offers unique experiences throughout the year. However, here are some general guidelines to help you choose the best time for your trip:

1. **Spring (March-May):** Spring is a delightful time to visit York, as the weather is generally mild and the city's gardens and parks burst into bloom. The crowds are smaller compared to the summer months, and many attractions have extended opening hours. Spring also marks the beginning of the festival season, with events like the York Festival of Ideas and the York Open Studios offering an array of cultural experiences.

2. **Summer (June-August):** Summer is the peak tourist season in York, with warm temperatures and long daylight hours, ideal for sightseeing and outdoor activities. However, be prepared for larger crowds at popular attractions and higher prices for accommodation. Summer also brings a host of festivals and events, including the York Races, the York Early Music Festival, and the Great Yorkshire Fringe.

3. **Autumn (September-November):** Autumn is another excellent time to visit York, as the weather remains relatively mild and the fall foliage adds a touch of beauty to the city's historic streets. The crowds begin to thin out after the busy summer months, and accommodation prices tend to be more affordable. Autumn also hosts some popular events, such as the York Food and Drink Festival and the Aesthetica Short Film Festival, which showcase the city's culinary and artistic talents.

4. **Winter (December-February):** Winter in York can be cold and wet, but the city takes on a magical atmosphere, particularly during the festive season. The York Christmas Market is a must-visit event, offering seasonal treats and unique gift ideas. Winter is also the quietest time to visit, with fewer tourists and lower accommodation prices. If you don't mind the colder weather, you can take advantage of

the peaceful atmosphere and explore the city's attractions at a leisurely pace.

In summary, the best time to visit York depends on your preferences for weather, crowd levels, and events. While spring and autumn offer a pleasant balance of mild temperatures, fewer crowds, and exciting festivals, summer and winter each have their own unique charms and experiences. Regardless of when you choose to visit, York promises a memorable and enchanting experience.

2.2 Entry Requirements and Visas

Before planning your trip to York, it is important to understand the entry requirements and visa regulations for the United Kingdom (UK). These requirements vary depending on your nationality and the purpose of your visit.

- EU, EEA, and Swiss Citizens: As of 2021, due to Brexit, EU, EEA, and Swiss citizens can visit the UK for short stays (up to 6 months) without a visa for tourism, family visits, or short-term business activities. However, they will need a visa for longer stays or if they plan to work or study in the UK. EU, EEA, and Swiss citizens must use a valid passport to enter the UK, as national ID cards are no longer accepted.

- Citizens of Visa-Exempt Countries: Citizens of some non-EU countries, such as the United States, Canada, Australia, New Zealand, and Japan, do not need a visa for short stays in the UK (up to 6 months) for tourism, family visits, or short-term business activities. A valid passport is required for entry.

- Citizens of Other Countries: Travelers from other countries may need to apply for a Standard Visitor Visa before visiting the UK. This visa allows for a stay of up to 6 months for tourism, family visits, or short-term business activities. To apply, you must submit an online application and provide supporting documents, such as a valid passport, proof of financial support, and details of your travel plans. It is recommended to apply for a visa well in advance of your trip, as processing times can vary.

- Additional Requirements: All travelers entering the UK may be subject to additional entry requirements, such as providing proof of a negative COVID-19 test, vaccination status, or completing a passenger locator form. Be sure to check the latest UK government guidance for any updates on these requirements before your trip.

It is essential to verify the specific entry requirements and visa regulations for your nationality before planning your visit to York. Information can be found on the UK government's official website or by contacting your local British embassy or consulate. Ensuring you have the appropriate documentation and meet the entry requirements will help ensure a smooth arrival and enjoyable stay in York.

2.3 Budgeting for Your Trip
York offers a variety of experiences for travelers with different budgets. To help you plan your trip, here are some general guidelines and tips for estimating your expenses while visiting York:

1. **Accommodation:** The cost of accommodation in York varies depending on your preferences and the time of year. Budget travelers can find hostels and budget hotels for around £20-40 per night, while mid-range hotels and B&Bs range from £60-120 per night. Luxury hotels and boutique accommodations can cost upwards of £150 per night. Booking in advance and considering off-peak travel times can help you secure the best deals.
2. **Food and drink:** Dining costs in York can range from inexpensive street food and pub meals (£8-15) to mid-range restaurants (£20-40 per person) and fine dining establishments (£50+ per person). For budget travelers, consider self-catering or visiting local markets to purchase

fresh produce and snacks. Don't forget to factor in the cost of drinks, which can be £3-6 for a pint of beer or £5-10 for a glass of wine in most establishments.

3. **Attractions:** Many of York's attractions charge an admission fee, typically ranging from £5-20 per person. To save money, consider purchasing a York Pass, which provides access to over 30 attractions for a fixed price, starting at £48 for a one-day adult pass. Some attractions, like the city walls and certain museums, offer free admission, allowing you to explore the city's history and culture without breaking the bank.

4. **Transportation:** York is a compact city, and many of its attractions are within walking distance. However, if you need to use public transportation, a single bus ticket costs around £2-3, while a day pass can be purchased for around £5. Taxis and rideshares are available, but they can be more expensive, with fares starting at £5-10 for short journeys. Biking is another budget-friendly option, with bike rentals starting at around £10 per day.

5. **Shopping and souvenirs**: York offers a variety of shopping options, from high-street brands and shopping centres to independent boutiques and markets. Souvenirs and local crafts can range from a few pounds for postcards and small trinkets to £20+ for handmade items or artwork. Budget accordingly for any shopping you plan to do while visiting York.

6. **Day trips and excursions:** York's location in the heart of Yorkshire makes it an ideal base for exploring the surrounding countryside and attractions. Day trips can vary in cost, with guided tours ranging from £30-80 per person, depending on the destination and duration of the tour. If you prefer to explore independently, consider renting a car or using public transportation to visit nearby attractions, such as the North York Moors National Park, the Yorkshire Dales, or the coastal town of Whitby. Keep in mind that transportation, admission fees, and dining costs will need to be factored into your budget for day trips.

7. **Miscellaneous expenses:** Remember to budget for any additional expenses, such as travel insurance, gratuities, and potential fees for Wi-Fi or mobile data usage. It's always a good idea to have some extra cash on hand for unexpected expenses or emergencies.

When budgeting for your trip to York, consider your travel style, interests, and priorities. By researching costs in advance and making informed decisions, you can create a budget that allows you to fully enjoy your York experience without overspending.

Getting to York

3.1 By Air

York does not have its own international airport, but there are several nearby airports with convenient connections to the city.

If you're coming from outside the UK, your best option is to **fly** to **Manchester Airport,** which is just over 80 miles away. Arguably, **Leeds/Bradford Airport** is closer if you're intending to hire a car, but if you're looking to use public transport, then Manchester is more convenient, as it has its own railway station. If you're intending to visit other parts of the UK as well as York, it may be better to fly to one of the London Airports (**Heathrow** is the most convenient in terms of public transport) and then use London as a hub for getting yourself elsewhere.

Here are the main airports to consider when planning your trip to York:

1. **Leeds Bradford Airport (LBA):** Located approximately 31 miles (50 km) from York, Leeds Bradford Airport is the closest major airport to the city. It offers flights to and from various destinations in Europe and the UK. To reach York from Leeds Bradford Airport, you can take a direct bus (the 747 Airport Shuttle) to York city center, which takes around 1 hour and 15 minutes. Alternatively, you can take a taxi or rent a car for the 50-minute drive.
2. **Manchester Airport (MAN):** Manchester Airport, situated around 85 miles (137 km) from York, is the largest international airport in the North of England. It serves a wide range of destinations across Europe, North America, and Asia. From Manchester Airport, you can take a direct train to York, with a journey time of approximately 1 hour and 50 minutes. Car rentals and taxis are also available for the 1 hour and 45-minute drive.
3. **Doncaster Sheffield Airport (DSA):** Doncaster Sheffield Airport is another option, located about 45 miles (72 km) from York. It offers flights to and from various European destinations. To get to York, you can take a bus or train from the airport to Doncaster, and then transfer to a direct train to York, with a total journey time of approximately 1 hour and 30 minutes. Car rentals and taxis are also available for the 1 hour and 15-minute drive.

4. **Newcastle Airport (NCL):** Newcastle Airport is located around 96 miles (155 km) from York and serves a variety of destinations in Europe and beyond. To reach York from Newcastle Airport, you can take the Tyne and Wear Metro to Newcastle Central Station and then catch a direct train to York, with a total journey time of approximately 2 hours and 15 minutes. Alternatively, you can rent a car or take a taxi for the 2-hour drive.
5. **London Airports:** If you're arriving from outside Europe or from a destination not served by the airports mentioned above, you may need to fly into one of London's airports, such as Heathrow (LHR), Gatwick (LGW), or Stansted (STN). From London, you can take a direct train to York from London King's Cross Station, with a journey time of around 2 hours. Alternatively, you can book a connecting flight from London to one of the airports closer to York, such as Manchester or Leeds Bradford.

Once you arrive at your chosen airport, consider using public transportation, taxis, or car rentals to complete the final leg of your journey to York.

3.2 By Train

York Railway Station. Photo: Michael D. Beckwith

Traveling to York by train is a convenient and comfortable option, with excellent rail connections to many cities across the UK. York Railway Station is centrally located, making it easy to access the city center and main attractions upon arrival.

1. **From London:** Direct trains from London King's Cross Station to York are operated by London North Eastern Railway (LNER) and take approximately 2 hours. Trains run frequently throughout the day, with up to 30 services available. Be sure to book your tickets in advance to secure the best fares.

2. **From Manchester:** Direct trains from Manchester Piccadilly Station to York are operated by TransPennine Express, with a journey time of around 1 hour and 20 minutes. Services run hourly throughout the day.

3. **From Edinburgh:** Direct trains from Edinburgh Waverley Station to York are operated by LNER and CrossCountry, taking around 2 hours and 30 minutes. Trains run frequently, with up to 20 services per day.

4. **From Birmingham:** Direct trains from Birmingham New Street Station to York are operated by CrossCountry, with a journey time of approximately 2 hours and 10 minutes. Services are available every hour.

5. **From Liverpool:** Direct trains from Liverpool Lime Street Station to York are operated by TransPennine Express and Northern, taking around 1 hour and 50 minutes. Services run hourly throughout the day.

The best place to buy train tickets is at the website for Virgin Trains East Coast. Tickets are available up to three months in advance, and this website offers tickets for trains across the country, not just for those operated by Virgin.

Tip: It is ALWAYS advised to book train tickets in England IN ADVANCE, because prices are much higher if you buy on the train directly from the ticket officer.

To book train tickets and check schedules, you can visit the National Rail website or the websites of the individual train operators. Booking in advance can often save you money, with discounted fares available for those who purchase tickets weeks or even months ahead of their travel date. Additionally, consider investing in a railcard if you plan to do extensive train travel in the UK, as it can provide significant savings on fares.

When traveling by train in the UK, it is essential to be aware of peak and off-peak travel times. Peak times generally occur during the morning and evening rush hours, when ticket prices are higher. If your schedule allows, traveling during off-peak hours can help you save money and enjoy a less crowded journey.

Upon arrival at York Railway Station, you will find a range of facilities, including ticket offices, luggage storage, shops, and cafes. The station is just a short walk from the city center, with many of York's top attractions within walking distance. Alternatively, you can catch a local bus or taxi from the station to reach your accommodation or explore further afield.

3.3 By Bus

If you're looking for a cheap but less comfortable form of transport, York is served by the **MegaBus**, which offers by far the cheapest ways of getting around the UK.

Traveling to York by bus is an affordable and eco-friendly option, with several long-distance coach services connecting the city to other destinations in the UK. While bus travel can be slower than train travel, it is often more budget-friendly, making it an attractive choice for cost-conscious travelers.

National Express: National Express is the largest long-distance coach operator in the UK, offering services to York from various cities such as London, Manchester, Birmingham, and Newcastle. Coaches arrive at the York Central Coach Station, which is conveniently located in the city center, close to many attractions and accommodations. Journey times vary depending on the route, with the trip from London to York taking approximately 4 to 5 hours. Booking in advance and traveling during off-peak times can help secure the best fares.

Megabus: Megabus is another popular coach operator in the UK, providing budget-friendly travel options to York from cities like London, Manchester, and Newcastle. Megabus services arrive at the York Leeman Road Coach Stop, which is a short walk from the city center and York Railway Station. Journey times are similar to those of National Express, with the trip from London taking around 4 to 5 hours. To get the best deals, book your tickets early and be flexible with your travel dates.

Local bus services: In addition to long-distance coach services, local buses provide an affordable and convenient way to travel within York and the surrounding areas. The city's bus network is operated by First York, offering a range of routes and services to various destinations. Single bus fares start at around £2-3, with day passes available for around £5. Be sure to check the bus schedules and routes before you travel, as services may vary depending on the time of day and day of the week.

3.4 By Car

If you intend to **drive** or hire a car, we recommend checking with your accommodation first to see if they have a car park. Otherwise, you may struggle to find a city centre car park that allows you to leave your car overnight.

Traveling to York by car is a flexible and convenient option, especially if you plan to explore the surrounding countryside and attractions. The city is easily accessible via major motorways, and there are several car rental options available at airports and in the city center.

From London: York is approximately 205 miles (330 km) from London, and the journey takes around 4 hours via the M1 and A1(M) motorways. Traffic can be heavy during peak hours, so it is advisable to avoid rush hour and plan your route in advance.

From Manchester: York is approximately 70 miles (113 km) from Manchester, and the journey takes around 1 hour and 20 minutes via the M62 and A64 motorways. Again, be aware of peak traffic times and plan accordingly.

From Edinburgh: York is approximately 220 miles (354 km) from Edinburgh, and the journey takes around 4 hours via the A1(M) motorway. The route is scenic, passing through beautiful countryside and charming towns.

Parking: There are several car parks located in the city center, including NCP car parks, which offer both short-term and long-term parking options. Street parking is also available, but can be limited and often requires payment during certain times of the day. Be sure to check parking regulations and fees before leaving your vehicle.

It is important to note that driving in the UK follows left-hand traffic, and drivers need to be familiar with UK road rules and signage. An international driving permit may be required for non-UK license holders.

Accommodation

4.1 Hotels

York offers a wide range of hotels to suit every budget and preference, from historic properties to modern and luxurious accommodations. Here are some of the top hotel options in the city:

The Grand, York: The Grand is a luxurious hotel housed in a historic Edwardian building that was once the headquarters of the North Eastern Railway. The hotel features elegant rooms and suites, a spa, and several dining options, including the 3 AA Rosette restaurant Hudson's. Prices start at around £200 per night. (Website: https://www.thegrandyork.co.uk/)

The Principal York: The Principal York is a stylish hotel located within walking distance of the city center and York Railway Station. The hotel features spacious rooms, a fitness center, and a restaurant serving modern British cuisine. Prices start at around £100 per night. (Website: https://www.phcompany.com/principal/york-hotel/)

Middletons Hotel: Middletons is a charming hotel set in a row of converted Georgian townhouses, located just outside the city walls. The hotel offers comfortable rooms, a bar, and a restaurant serving British classics. Prices start at around £70 per night. (Website: https://www.middletonsyork.co.uk/)

The Mount Royale Hotel & Spa: The Mount Royale is a family-run hotel located in a Victorian mansion, surrounded by lush gardens. The hotel offers spacious rooms, a spa, and a restaurant serving locally sourced cuisine. Prices start at around £80 per night. (Website: https://www.mountroyale.co.uk/)

The Churchill Hotel: The Churchill is a boutique hotel set in a restored Georgian mansion, located within walking distance of the city center and York Minster. The hotel features individually decorated rooms, a restaurant, and a cocktail bar. Prices start at around £100 per night. (https://www.churchillhotel.com/)

4.2 Bed & Breakfasts

Bed & Breakfasts (B&Bs) are a popular accommodation option in York, offering a more personal and traditional experience for travelers. Here are some recommended B&Bs in York:

The Bloomsbury: This family-run B&B is located in a quiet residential area, just a 15-minute walk from York city center. The Bloomsbury offers elegantly decorated rooms with en-suite bathrooms and modern amenities such as flat-screen TVs and free Wi-Fi. A hearty English breakfast is included in the room rate. Prices start at around £85 per night. Website: https://thebloomsburyguesthouseyork.co.uk/

The Crescent Guest House: This charming Victorian townhouse is situated in a leafy residential area, just a 10-minute walk from York Minster. The Crescent Guest House offers individually decorated rooms with en-suite bathrooms, as well as a guest lounge and garden. A full English breakfast is served each morning. Prices start at around £70 per night. Website: https://www.crescentguesthouse.co.uk/

Gillygate Guest House: This award-winning B&B is located in the heart of York, just a short walk from the city's main attractions and shopping areas. Gillygate Guest House offers comfortable rooms with en-suite bathrooms, as well as a guest lounge and garden. A full English breakfast is included in the room rate. Prices start at around £90 per night. Website: https://www.gillygateguesthouse.co.uk/

No. 21 York: This stylish B&B is housed in a Grade II listed Georgian townhouse, just a 10-minute walk from York city center. No. 21 York offers elegantly decorated rooms with en-suite bathrooms, as well as a guest lounge and garden. A continental breakfast is included in the room rate. Prices start at around £110 per night. Website: https://www.no21york.co.uk/

4.3 Hostels

Hostels are a great option for budget travelers looking to save money on accommodation while still enjoying comfortable and convenient lodgings. York has several hostels that offer affordable rates and a range of amenities for guests. Here are a few options to consider:

YHA York Hostel - Located in a beautiful Victorian mansion just a short walk from the city center, YHA York Hostel offers dormitory and private rooms with shared bathroom facilities. The hostel features a self-catering kitchen, a cozy lounge with a fireplace, and a bar serving local beers and spirits. Prices start at around £16 per person per night for a dormitory room.

Safestay York - Set in a stunning Georgian townhouse, Safestay York offers a mix of private and dormitory rooms, all with en suite bathrooms. The hostel features a shared lounge, a garden, and a bar serving cocktails and light bites. The property is just a 10-minute walk from York Minster and other major attractions. Prices start at around £14 per person per night for a dormitory room.

Fort Boutique Hostel - Fort Boutique Hostel is a unique and quirky hostel located within a historic fortification in the heart of York. The hostel offers a mix of private and dormitory rooms, all with en suite bathrooms and stylish decor. The property features a lounge with a fireplace, a courtyard garden, and a bar serving drinks and snacks. Prices start at around £25 per person per night for a dormitory room.

The Red Lion - This cozy and friendly hostel is located just a few steps from York Railway Station and offers a mix of private and dormitory rooms with shared bathroom facilities. The hostel features a communal kitchen, a lounge area, and a garden with outdoor seating. Prices start at around £15 per person per night for a dormitory room.

All of these hostels offer free Wi-Fi, luggage storage, and 24-hour reception. Be sure to book in advance, especially during peak season, to secure the best rates and availability.

4.4 Self-Catering and Apartments

If you're looking for more independence and flexibility during your stay in York, self-catering apartments can be an excellent choice. Here are some options to consider:

1. **The Lawrance Luxury ApartHotel** - This award-winning apartment hotel is located in the heart of York, just a few minutes' walk from many of the city's main attractions. The apartments range in size from studios to two-bedroom units, all of which are stylishly decorated and well-equipped for self-catering stays. Prices start from around £115 per night. You can find more information and book on their website: https://www.lawranceapartments.co.uk/

2. **Staycity Aparthotels Paragon Street** - Situated just a 10-minute walk from York Railway Station, Staycity Aparthotels offers spacious, modern apartments with fully equipped kitchens and living areas. The apartments are available in a range of sizes, from studios to two-bedroom units, and prices start from around £80 per night. You can find more information and book on their website: https://www.staycity.com/york/paragon-street/

3. **Goodramgate Apartments** - These stylish apartments are located in the heart of York's historic center, just a few steps from the famous Shambles. The apartments are well-appointed and come with fully equipped kitchens, living areas, and free Wi-Fi. Prices start from around £100 per night. You can find more information and book on their website: https://goodramgateapartments.com/

4. **The Grand York Residences** - Situated in the grand surroundings of the Grade II-listed former North Eastern Railway headquarters, The Grand York Residences offer luxurious self-catering apartments with all the amenities of a five-star hotel. The apartments are available in a range of sizes, from studios to three-bedroom units, and prices start from around £200 per night. You can find more information

and book on their website:
https://www.thegrandyork.co.uk/residences/

4.5 Unique Stays

If you're looking for a unique accommodation experience in York, there are plenty of options to choose from. Here are some ideas:

1. YHA York: This historic youth hostel is housed in a 13th-century building and offers affordable dormitory and private rooms. It's located within the city walls, close to the main attractions. Prices start at around £20 per night.
2. The Grand Hotel & Spa: For a luxurious stay, consider The Grand Hotel & Spa, housed in a former Victorian railway building. The hotel features elegant rooms and suites, a spa, and a rooftop bar with stunning views of the city. Prices start at around £150 per night.
3. The Boatel: This unique accommodation option offers guests the chance to stay on a converted barge on the River Ouse. The Boatel features a cozy cabin with a double bed, kitchenette, and bathroom facilities. Prices start at around £100 per night.
4. Middlethorpe Hall & Spa: For a historic stay in a country house setting, consider Middlethorpe Hall & Spa. This 17th-century mansion is set in 20 acres of gardens and parkland and features elegant rooms, a spa, and an award-winning restaurant. Prices start at around £200 per night.
5. The Bivouac: This eco-friendly glamping site offers guests the chance to stay in stylish yurts or cabins in the nearby countryside. The Bivouac features a communal barn with a cafe and a shop selling local produce. Prices start at around £100 per night.

To book any of these unique stays, visit their websites for more information and availability.

4.6 Our Top Suggestions

Budget Option

Hostels aren't cheap in England, so your best bet is <u>The Fort Boutique Hostel.</u> With dorm rooms from £18 per night, free laundry service, free toiletries, occasionally free drinks… Just be aware that there's a large bar beneath the hostel that will keep you awake if you're not a party animal.

Mid-Range Option

A bed-and-breakfast is your best option in the midrange category, and the most convenient, especially if you have a motor, is the <u>Heworth Guest House.</u> Located about a mile away from the city centre in an area with no parking restrictions, the place has recently undergone a refurbishment and at around £40 per night, it's difficult to find anywhere for better value.

Splurge Option

If you want to spend all your money, why not head over to <u>Middlethorpe Hall</u>? Single rooms from £139, doubles from £199. It's a 17th century country house with a spa, 8 acres of land, individually decorated rooms with original antiques, and bursting with charm. The best option to have everything you could possibly want.

Transportation in York

5.1 Public Transport

York has a reliable and affordable public transportation system, which includes buses and trains. The bus network in York is operated by First York, and tickets can be purchased on board or through the First Bus app. A single bus ticket costs around £2-3, while a day pass can be purchased for around £5. York also has a Park & Ride system, which offers convenient and affordable parking on the outskirts of the city, with regular bus services to the city center.

Trains are another convenient option for getting around York and the surrounding areas. York Railway Station is a major transportation hub, with frequent services to major cities like London, Edinburgh, Manchester, and Birmingham. The TransPennine Express and LNER are the main train operators serving York.

5.2 Taxis and Rideshares

Taxis and rideshares are widely available in York, offering a convenient and comfortable option for getting around the city. Taxis can be hailed on the street, or booked in advance through local companies such as Streamline Taxis, York Cars, and Fleetways Taxis. Fares vary depending on the distance traveled and time of day, but a typical fare for a short journey within the city center would be around £5-10.

Rideshare services like Uber and Bolt are also available in York, offering competitive rates and convenience for travelers. These services can be booked through their respective apps, with fares calculated based on distance and time.

5.3 Biking

Biking is a convenient and eco-friendly way to explore York, and there are several bike rental companies in the city. Some of the most popular routes for cycling include the York Solar System Cycleway, which takes you on a 6.4-mile (10.3 km) journey through the city's green spaces, and the York to Selby Cycle Path, which follows the River Ouse and offers scenic views of the countryside.

Prices for bike rentals in York vary depending on the type of bike and the duration of the rental. A standard hybrid bike can be rented for around £15-20 per day, while an electric bike can cost around £30-40 per day. Many bike rental companies also offer guided tours and self-guided routes to help you make the most of your cycling experience in York.

5.4 Walking

York is a compact city, and many of its attractions are within easy walking distance of each other. Walking is an excellent way to explore the city's narrow, winding streets and discover its hidden gems. The city also offers several guided walking tours, such as the York Ghost Walk and the York Walls Walk, which provide a unique perspective on the city's history and culture.

York's historic city center is pedestrian-friendly, with many of its streets closed to traffic. This creates a relaxed and charming atmosphere that is perfect for leisurely strolls and exploration. Walking tours can range from free self-guided options to paid tours with professional guides, with prices starting at around £5-10 per person.

York's Top Attractions

York is home to a wealth of top-rated attractions that showcase the city's rich history and culture. Here are just a few of the must-see sights and experiences:

6.1 York Minster: One of the largest and most impressive cathedrals in Northern Europe, York Minster is a masterpiece of Gothic architecture. The cathedral dates back to the 7th century and features stunning stained glass windows, intricate stonework, and a towering central tower with stunning views of the city. Visitors can explore the cathedral's interior, attend services, or take guided tours to learn more about its history and significance.

6.2 The Shambles: A picturesque medieval street in the heart of York, the Shambles is lined with quaint shops, restaurants, and charming buildings that date back to the 14th century. Its unique architecture and narrow lanes make it one of the most photographed streets in the city. The Shambles is also home to the world-famous Harry Potter-themed shop, The Shop That Must Not Be Named.

6.3 York City Walls: The city walls are an iconic feature of York, dating back to Roman times. They stretch for 2.5 miles around the city center, providing breathtaking views of the city's historic buildings and landmarks. Walking along the walls is a popular activity for visitors and locals alike.

6.4 Jorvik Viking Centre: Experience Viking history firsthand at the Jorvik Viking Centre, an immersive museum that showcases the sights, sounds, and smells of Viking-era York. Visitors can ride through recreated Viking streets and homes, see artifacts from the era, and learn about Viking life and culture.

6.5 National Railway Museum: Train enthusiasts will love the National Railway Museum, which houses an impressive collection of historic locomotives, including the iconic Flying

Scotsman. The museum also offers interactive exhibits, hands-on activities, and train rides for visitors of all ages.

6.6 York Castle Museum: Located in a former prison, the York Castle Museum features exhibits that tell the story of York's history and culture, from the Victorian era to the present day. Visitors can explore recreated period rooms, see historic costumes, and learn about the lives of ordinary people throughout history.

6.7 Clifford's Tower: This 13th-century tower is one of the most iconic landmarks in York. Located on a hill overlooking the city, it offers stunning views of the surrounding countryside. Visitors can explore the tower's history and climb to the top for panoramic views of York.

6.8 The York Dungeon: For a more unique and immersive experience, visit the York Dungeon, which offers interactive exhibits and live actors that bring York's dark history to life. Visitors can journey through York's past, from the Viking era to the infamous Guy Fawkes plot, in a theatrical and entertaining way.

6.9 York Art Gallery: Art lovers will appreciate the York Art Gallery, which houses an impressive collection of paintings, ceramics, and sculptures from around the world. The museum's permanent collection includes works by local artists, as well as pieces by internationally renowned artists such as David Hockney and L.S. Lowry.

6.10 York Maze: Located just outside the city, York Maze is a fun-filled attraction that offers family-friendly activities, including a giant maze made from maize, a miniature golf course, and a petting zoo. Visitors can spend hours exploring the maze and enjoying the other attractions on offer.

Hidden Gems and Lesser-Known Attractions

7.1 Barley Hall: This beautifully restored medieval townhouse transports visitors back to the 15th century. It features stunning period furnishings and decorations, providing a glimpse into the lives of wealthy merchants during the Middle Ages. Visitors can enjoy interactive exhibits, try on medieval clothing, and learn about the history of the building. Website: https://www.barleyhall.org.uk/ Admission: Adult £9.50, Child £5.50.

7.2 Treasurer's House: Located in the heart of York, Treasurer's House is a historic townhouse with a fascinating past. It was once home to the treasurers of York Minster and is now a museum filled with art, antiques, and curiosities. Visitors can explore the house and its beautiful gardens, as well as learn about its ghostly legends. Website: https://www.nationaltrust.org.uk/treasurers-house-york Admission: Adult £8.60, Child £4.30.

7.3 The Cold War Bunker: This hidden gem is a former nuclear bunker located beneath York's historic streets. Built in the 1960s as part of the UK's Cold War defense strategy, the bunker was designed to protect key officials and personnel in the event of a nuclear attack. Visitors can take a guided tour of the bunker and learn about its history and operations. Website: https://www.english-heritage.org.uk/visit/places/york-cold-war-bunker/ Admission: Adult £10.50, Child £6.30.

7.4 Holy Trinity Church, Goodramgate: This small, unassuming church is tucked away in the heart of York's city center. It is believed to be the oldest medieval church in York, dating back to the 11th century. Visitors can admire its unique architecture and stained glass windows, as well as learn about its fascinating history. Admission is free, although donations are appreciated.

7.5 The Snickleways of York: Snickleways are a network of narrow, winding alleyways that crisscross York's historic center.

These hidden paths offer a glimpse into the city's medieval past, with many dating back to the 14th century. Visitors can explore the snickleways on foot and discover hidden courtyards, ancient landmarks, and charming hidden corners. Maps of the snickleways are available at the Visit York Information Center. Admission is free.

Food and Drink

8.1 Traditional Yorkshire Cuisine

Yorkshire has a rich culinary heritage, and trying some of its traditional dishes is a must for any visitor. Here are some of the most popular Yorkshire dishes to look out for:

- Yorkshire pudding: A savory baked pudding made from a batter of eggs, flour, and milk or water. It's usually served with roast beef and gravy, but can also be eaten as a snack or as a dessert with fruit and cream.
- Roast beef: A classic Sunday roast featuring tender slices of beef served with vegetables and gravy.
- Wensleydale cheese: A crumbly, tangy cheese made from cow's milk and named after the Wensleydale region of Yorkshire.
- Parkin: A spicy gingerbread-like cake made with oats, molasses, and ginger.
- Fish and chips: A quintessentially British dish consisting of battered and fried fish served with thick-cut chips (fries) and mushy peas.

8.2 Local Pubs and Bars

York has a vibrant pub and bar scene, with many historic establishments dating back hundreds of years. Here are some of the top pubs and bars to visit while in York:

- The Golden Fleece: This historic pub, which dates back to the 16th century, is said to be one of the most haunted pubs in England. It's a cozy spot for a pint of real ale and some traditional pub food.
- The House of Trembling Madness: A unique and quirky pub and shop selling an extensive range of beer, wine, and spirits from around the world. The pub is located above the shop and has a medieval-inspired decor.
- Ye Olde Starre Inn: Another historic pub, dating back to the 16th century, and known for its cozy atmosphere, real ale, and traditional pub grub.
- Evil Eye Lounge: A popular cocktail bar with a quirky decor and an extensive cocktail menu featuring creative and unusual concoctions.
- The Blue Bell: A traditional pub located just outside the city walls, known for its excellent selection of real ale and pub food.

8.3 Afternoon Tea

Afternoon tea is a quintessential British experience, and York has many establishments that offer this beloved tradition. From elegant tearooms to historic hotels, here are some of the best places to enjoy afternoon tea in York:

1. Betty's Cafe Tea Rooms: A York institution, Betty's Cafe Tea Rooms has been serving traditional afternoon tea since 1919. Located in the heart of the city center, this elegant tearoom offers a range of tea options, including their signature blend, as well as a selection of sandwiches, scones, and cakes.

2. The Grand Hotel & Spa: This historic hotel in the heart of York offers a luxurious afternoon tea experience in its stunning Grand Boardroom. Guests can enjoy a selection of finger sandwiches, freshly baked scones, and a range of pastries and cakes, all served on fine china.

3. Middlethorpe Hall & Spa: This 17th-century country house hotel just outside York offers a traditional afternoon tea served in their elegant Drawing Room or on the terrace overlooking the gardens. The menu features a selection of finger sandwiches, scones, and sweet treats, all accompanied by your choice of tea or coffee.

4. The Principal York: This iconic hotel in a converted Victorian railway station offers a delicious afternoon tea in its Garden Room, overlooking the hotel's private gardens. The menu features a selection of savory bites, freshly baked scones, and a range of sweet treats, accompanied by your choice of tea or coffee.

5. The Ivy St. Helen's Square: This stylish restaurant in the heart of York offers an elegant afternoon tea with a modern twist. The menu includes a selection of savory bites, freshly baked scones, and a range of sweet treats, all accompanied by your choice of tea or Champagne.

Whether you're looking for a traditional or modern twist on afternoon tea, York has something to suit all tastes and budgets. Be sure to book in advance, as many of these establishments can be quite popular and get fully booked quickly.

8.4 Fine Dining and Gourmet Experiences

York has a thriving food scene, with a range of gourmet experiences and fine dining options for visitors to enjoy. Here are some top recommendations:

1. Roots: A Michelin-starred restaurant, Roots offers a unique dining experience that showcases the best of local produce and ingredients. The menu is constantly changing, but expect innovative dishes that blend classic techniques with modern twists. Average price for a tasting menu is £75 per person.

2. The Park Restaurant by Adam Jackson: Located in the heart of York, this elegant restaurant offers contemporary British cuisine in a stylish setting. With an emphasis on fresh, seasonal ingredients and creative flavor combinations, The Park is a favorite among foodies and locals alike. Average price for a three-course meal is £45 per person.

3. Le Cochon Aveugle: This intimate French restaurant offers a tasting menu that changes weekly, featuring dishes made with locally sourced, seasonal ingredients. The menu is a surprise, with diners only finding out what they'll be eating as each course is served. Average price for a tasting menu is £65 per person.

4. Skosh: Skosh is a trendy, modern eatery that offers small plates with big flavors. The menu draws inspiration from around the world, with dishes like Korean fried chicken, smoked mackerel pate, and lamb kofta. Average price for a three-course meal is £35 per person.

5. The Ivy St. Helen's Square: The Ivy is a well-known chain of restaurants across the UK, but the York location is particularly special, housed in a historic building in the city center. The menu features classic British dishes with a modern twist, and the stylish decor adds to the overall experience. Average price for a three-course meal is £40 per person.

8.5 Vegetarian and Vegan Options

York is a city that caters to a variety of dietary preferences, including vegetarian and vegan options. Here are some top spots to check out for plant-based dining:

1. El Piano: This award-winning vegetarian and vegan restaurant serves up a creative menu of Mediterranean-inspired dishes. Their tapas and mezze plates are particularly popular. (Website: https://www.el-piano.com/, Average Price: £10-15 per person)
2. Goji Cafe: This vegan cafe offers a range of plant-based dishes, from sandwiches and salads to burgers and hot dishes. They also have a selection of vegan cakes and desserts. (Website: https://gojicafe.co.uk/, Average Price: £8-12 per person)
3. Source: This vegetarian cafe and health food shop focuses on fresh, locally sourced ingredients. They offer a variety of vegetarian and vegan options, including salads, sandwiches, and hot dishes. (Website: https://www.source-york.co.uk/, Average Price: £8-12 per person)
4. The Go Down: This vegetarian cafe and arts space serves up a range of plant-based dishes, including breakfast items, sandwiches, salads, and hot dishes. They also have a selection of vegan cakes and desserts. (Website: https://www.thegodown.co.uk/, Average Price: £8-12 per person)
5. Ambiente Tapas: This Spanish-inspired tapas bar offers a range of vegetarian and vegan options, including patatas bravas, pan con tomate, and grilled vegetables. (Website: https://www.ambiente-tapas.co.uk/, Average Price: £15-20 per person)

These are just a few of the many options for vegetarian and vegan dining in York.

8.6 International Cuisine

York's dining scene offers a diverse range of international cuisine, from Italian and Indian to Thai and Japanese. Here are some popular options for international dining in York:

1. Ambiente Tapas - This restaurant serves a variety of Spanish tapas dishes, including grilled meats, seafood, and vegetarian options. They also have an extensive wine list to complement the flavors of the dishes. Website: https://www.ambiente-tapas.co.uk/
2. Rustique - Rustique is a French restaurant located in the heart of York's city center. They offer a variety of classic French dishes such as Escargots de Bourgogne, Confit de Canard, and Coq au Vin. Website: https://www.rustiquerestaurants.co.uk/york
3. Los Moros - Los Moros is a Moroccan restaurant that serves a range of authentic Moroccan dishes, including tagines, mezze, and grilled meats. They also offer vegetarian and vegan options. Website: https://www.losmorosyork.co.uk/
4. Thai Season - This restaurant serves a range of traditional Thai dishes such as Pad Thai, Tom Yum soup, and Green Curry. They also offer vegetarian and vegan options. Website: https://www.thaiseason.co.uk/
5. The Yak & Yeti - The Yak & Yeti is a Nepalese and Indian restaurant located in the heart of York. They serve a range of traditional Nepalese and Indian dishes such as momos, curries, and tandoori dishes. They also offer vegetarian and vegan options. Website: https://www.yakandyeti.co.uk/

Shopping and Souvenirs

9.1 Independent Shops and Boutiques

York is home to a vibrant independent shopping scene, offering a range of unique and locally made items. The city's winding streets and historic buildings provide the perfect backdrop for browsing independent shops and boutiques. Some of the best places to explore include:

- Stonegate Teddy Bears: This charming shop on Stonegate specializes in handmade teddy bears, ranging from traditional designs to quirky and unique creations. Website: https://stonegateteddybears.co.uk/
- Hebden Tea: A tea-lover's paradise, Hebden Tea offers an extensive selection of loose leaf teas from around the world, as well as teapots, cups, and other accessories. Website: https://hebdentea.com/
- The Imaginarium: A whimsical gift shop on Blake Street, The Imaginarium sells a range of quirky and unusual items, from vintage-style toys to taxidermy and curiosities. Website: https://www.theimaginariumyork.co.uk/
- Hebden's Lucky Dip: This charming shop on Gillygate is filled with an eclectic mix of vintage and retro items, including clothing, jewelry, and homeware. The Lucky Dip element means you never know what you might find! Website: https://hebdensluckydip.co.uk/
- The York Gin Shop: Located in the heart of York, The York Gin Shop offers a range of locally distilled gins, as well as gin-inspired gifts and accessories. Website: https://www.yorkgin.com/shop

9.2 York's Markets

York is renowned for its bustling markets, offering a range of goods from fresh produce to handcrafted souvenirs. Some of the top markets to visit include:

- Shambles Market: Located on the historic Shambles street, this market offers a range of food stalls, artisanal crafts, and vintage finds. Open seven days a week. Website: https://www.shamblesmarket.com/

- York's Farmers' Market: Held on the first Friday of each month in Parliament Street, York's Farmers' Market showcases the best of local produce and food products. Website: https://www.yorkfarmersmarket.com/
- The Fleeting Arms Market: Held on the first Saturday of each month, this indoor market features local artists, makers, and designers, offering a range of unique and handmade items. Website: https://thefleetingarmsmarket.com/

9.3 Antique and Vintage Finds

York is a treasure trove for antique and vintage enthusiasts, with a range of shops and markets offering unique and one-of-a-kind finds. Some of the top spots to explore include:
- The Red House Antiques Centre: Housed in a former Victorian chapel, this antiques centre features over 30 dealers offering a range of antiques and vintage items. Website: https://www.redhouseyork.co.uk/
- The Antiques Centre York: Located on Stonegate, this antiques centre features four floors of dealers selling everything from antique furniture to vintage clothing and jewelry. Website: https://www.antiquescentreyork.co.uk/
- The York Emporium: A vintage-inspired cafe and bookstore, The York Emporium also features a range of vintage and antique items for sale, including books, records, and collectibles. Website: https://yorkemporium.co.uk/

9.4 Art Galleries and Craft Shops

In addition to independent shops and markets, York also has a selection of art galleries and craft shops that showcase the city's creative side. Here are some top picks:
According to Visit York, some popular galleries and craft shops in York include:
- According to McArthur Glen Designer Outlet York: This shopping center features over 120 designer and high street brands, including Polo Ralph Lauren, Ted Baker, and Calvin Klein. It's located just outside the city center and offers discounts up to 60% off all year round.

- The Coppergate Shopping Centre: This indoor shopping center features a mix of high street brands and independent retailers, including H&M, Next, and The Yorkshire Soap Company. It's conveniently located in the heart of the city center.
- The Shambles Market: In addition to the outdoor market stalls selling local produce and crafts, the Shambles Market also features a number of independent shops and artisanal food vendors. It's a great place to browse for unique souvenirs and gifts.
- The York Art Gallery: This museum features an impressive collection of paintings, ceramics, and other works of art from around the world. The gallery also hosts regular exhibitions and events throughout the year.
- According to Visit York, some other notable galleries and craft shops in York include Blossom Street Gallery, Lotte Inch Gallery, and Pyramid Gallery.

Whether you're looking for designer labels, local produce, or unique works of art, York has plenty of shopping options to explore.

9.5 Shopping Centres and High Street Brands

York offers a mix of independent shops and high street brands, providing a range of shopping experiences to suit different tastes and budgets. Here are some of the main shopping centres and high street brands in York:

1. Coppergate Shopping Centre: Located in the heart of York, Coppergate Shopping Centre is a modern indoor shopping centre with over 30 stores, including popular brands like H&M, Next, and Boots.
2. Vangarde Shopping Park: Vangarde Shopping Park is a popular retail destination located just outside the city centre. It features a mix of high street brands like Marks & Spencer, John Lewis, and Outfit, as well as restaurants and a cinema.
3. Coney Street: Coney Street is one of York's main shopping streets, lined with a mix of high street and independent shops. Popular brands include Topshop, River Island, and Superdry.

4. The Shambles Market: The Shambles Market offers a mix of food, drink, and shopping stalls, selling everything from local produce to artisan crafts and souvenirs.
5. Monks Cross Shopping Park: Monks Cross Shopping Park is a large retail park just outside the city centre, featuring popular brands like Primark, TK Maxx, and Sainsbury's.

Whether you're looking for the latest fashion trends or unique souvenirs to take home, York has something for every shopper.

Day Trips and Excursions

10.1 North York Moors National Park

A scenic destination for nature lovers, the North York Moors National Park is located just a short drive from York. This vast and varied landscape offers stunning vistas of rolling hills, rugged coastline, and ancient woodlands, as well as a chance to see local wildlife and explore historic villages. Visitors can enjoy activities such as hiking, cycling, and horseback riding, as well as visiting popular attractions like the North York Moors Railway and the ruined Rievaulx Abbey.

10.2 Yorkshire Dales

Another popular day trip from York is a visit to the Yorkshire Dales, an area of stunning natural beauty that is renowned for its sweeping landscapes, picturesque villages, and traditional farming communities. The Dales offer a range of outdoor activities, from hiking and cycling to rock climbing and caving, as well as a chance to visit historic sites such as Bolton Castle and Aysgarth Falls. Visitors can also sample local food and drink, including traditional Yorkshire puddings, Wensleydale cheese, and local ale.

10.3 Castle Howard

Castle Howard is a magnificent stately home located about 15 miles (24 km) north of York. The house boasts stunning architecture and interiors, including a world-famous Great Hall, impressive art collections, and beautiful gardens. Visitors can explore the house and grounds, enjoy afternoon tea, and participate in various events and exhibitions throughout the year. Website: https://www.castlehoward.co.uk/. Admission prices start at £19 for adults.

10.4 Fountains Abbey and Studley Royal Water Garden

Fountains Abbey and Studley Royal Water Garden is a UNESCO World Heritage site located about 20 miles (32 km) north of York. The abbey ruins and the 18th-century water garden are set in a picturesque valley, offering a tranquil and atmospheric setting for a day trip. Visitors can explore the ruins, take a stroll in the gardens, and enjoy the scenic views. Website: https://www.nationaltrust.org.uk/fountains-abbey-and-studley-royal-water-garden. Admission prices start at £16.50 for adults.

10.5 Whitby and the Yorkshire Coast

Whitby is a charming seaside town located about 50 miles (80 km) east of York. It is famous for its historic abbey ruins, Gothic architecture, and association with Bram Stoker's Dracula. Visitors can explore the town's winding streets, picturesque harbor, and beaches, as well as sample the local seafood and fish and chips. The Yorkshire Coast offers stunning views, quaint villages, and historic sites, such as Scarborough Castle and Filey Brigg.

10.6 Harrogate and Ripon

Harrogate and Ripon are two elegant towns located about 20 miles (32 km) west of York. They are known for their spa heritage, beautiful gardens, and charming architecture. Visitors can enjoy a leisurely stroll through the Valley Gardens, explore the Turkish Baths, and sample the famous Betty's Tea Rooms. Ripon is home to the stunning Cathedral Church of St. Peter and St. Wilfrid, and the ancient Ripon Racecourse.

10.7 The City of Leeds

Leeds is a vibrant and cosmopolitan city located about 25 miles (40 km) south-west of York. It offers a mix of modern and historic attractions, including the Royal Armouries Museum, the Leeds Art Gallery, and the Victorian shopping arcades. Visitors can also explore the city's diverse neighborhoods, such as the trendy Northern Quarter, the bohemian Hyde Park, and the student area of Headingley.

10.8 The Brontë Parsonage and Haworth

The Brontë Parsonage is a historic house museum located in the village of Haworth, about 30 miles (48 km) west of York. It was the home of the famous Brontë sisters, who wrote some of the most beloved novels in English literature. Visitors can explore the house, the surrounding moors, and the village, which still retains its charming 19th-century character. Website: https://www.bronte.org.uk/. Admission prices start at £10.50 for adults.

Festivals and Events

11.1 York Festival of Ideas

This annual event, held in June, celebrates ideas, debate, and the exchange of knowledge. It features a range of talks, workshops, and performances on various topics, from science and technology to arts and humanities. Check out their website for the latest program and ticket information.

11.2 York Food and Drink Festival

This festival, held in September, celebrates the best of York's culinary scene, with local food and drink producers showcasing their products in various locations across the city. The festival also includes cooking demonstrations, talks, and workshops. Admission to most events is free, but some may require tickets.

11.3 York Races

York Racecourse hosts several horse racing events throughout the year, with the highlight being the Ebor Festival in August. The festival attracts top horses, jockeys, and trainers from around the world and features four days of thrilling racing and entertainment.

11.4 York Christmas Market

The York Christmas Market, held in November and December, is a festive extravaganza, featuring over 100 stalls selling gifts, crafts, and food and drink. The market is set in York's historic streets and features live music and entertainment, making it a perfect way to get into the holiday spirit.

11.5 York Literature Festival

This festival, held in March, celebrates the written word and features a range of literary events, including talks, readings, and workshops. The festival attracts a mix of local and international writers, making it a must-attend event for book lovers.

11.6 JORVIK Viking Festival

This festival, held in February, celebrates York's Viking heritage with a range of events, including living history encampments, talks, workshops, and performances. The highlight of the festival is the dramatic finale, the Battle Spectacular, which features over 200 warriors and a spectacular firework display.

11.7 York Early Music Festival

This festival, held in July, celebrates early music from the medieval, Renaissance, and Baroque periods. It features performances from renowned international musicians, as well as workshops and talks. The festival takes place in various historic venues across the city, creating a unique and immersive experience for music lovers.

Nightlife and Entertainment

12.1 Theatre and Performing Arts

York is home to several theatres, showcasing a diverse range of productions, from classic plays to modern works. The York Theatre Royal is a popular venue, hosting plays, musicals, and other performances throughout the year. The Grand Opera House is another historic theatre in the city center, featuring a range of touring productions, comedians, and musical acts.

12.2 Live Music Venues

York boasts several live music venues, offering a mix of local and touring acts. The Crescent Community Venue is a popular spot, hosting a variety of genres, from indie and rock to jazz and folk. Fibbers is another well-known venue, known for its lively atmosphere and gigs by up-and-coming bands.

12.3 Cinemas

For film enthusiasts, York has several cinemas, including the City Screen Picturehouse, which shows a mix of independent and mainstream films. The Vue Cinema in the city center is another option, featuring the latest blockbusters.

12.4 Comedy Clubs

York has a thriving comedy scene, with several venues hosting regular stand-up comedy nights. The Basement is a popular spot, featuring up-and-coming comedians and established acts. The Great Yorkshire Fringe, held annually in July, also includes a range of comedy performances.

12.5 Dance Clubs and Bars

York's nightlife scene offers a mix of bars and clubs, catering to different tastes and preferences. Fibbers is not only a live music venue but also hosts regular club nights, playing a variety of music genres. The Mansion Nightclub is another popular spot, featuring different themed rooms and a rooftop terrace.

12.6 Ghost Walks and Haunted Experiences

York's rich history and ancient streets are the perfect setting for ghost walks and haunted experiences. Several companies offer tours, taking visitors on a spooky journey through the city's haunted past. The York Ghost Bus Tour is a fun and entertaining way to explore the city after dark.

Travel Tips and Safety

13.1 Health and Medical Services

York has a range of medical facilities, including hospitals, clinics, and pharmacies. If you need medical attention during your stay, you can call 111 for non-emergency medical advice or visit the York Hospital's Accident and Emergency Department (located on Wigginton Road). It is recommended to have travel insurance that covers medical emergencies.

13.2 Accessibility and Mobility

York's city center is largely accessible for people with mobility issues, with many attractions, restaurants, and shops offering wheelchair access. Some of the city's historic buildings may have limited accessibility, but there are often alternative routes or facilities available. York also has a wheelchair-friendly taxi service, Streamline Taxis.

13.3 Banking and Currency

The currency used in the UK is the British Pound (GBP). Banks and ATMs can be found throughout the city center, and most businesses accept major credit cards. It is a good idea to inform your bank of your travel plans to avoid any issues with accessing your funds.

13.4 Tipping and Gratuities

Tipping in the UK is generally discretionary, but a 10-15% tip is expected in restaurants and cafes for good service. It is also common to tip hairdressers, taxi drivers, and hotel staff.

13.5 Staying Connected: Wi-Fi and Mobile Services

Many restaurants, cafes, and public spaces offer free Wi-Fi, and most hotels and accommodations provide internet access. Mobile phone coverage is generally good in York, but be sure to check your provider's international roaming charges before using your phone abroad.

13.6 Local Customs and Etiquette

It is considered polite to say "please" and "thank you" when interacting with locals and service staff. Queueing is also an important aspect of British etiquette, and cutting in line is frowned upon. Smoking is prohibited in enclosed public spaces, including bars and restaurants. Drinking alcohol in public is legal in York but should be done responsibly.

13.7 Emergency Contacts and Services
In case of emergency in York, the following contacts and services are available:

- Police, Fire, and Ambulance: Dial 999 (or 112 from a mobile phone)
- Non-emergency police: Dial 101
- York Hospital: (01904) 631313
- NHS 111: Dial 111 for non-emergency medical advice
- York Samaritans: (01904) 655888 (24-hour helpline for emotional support)

13.8 Weather and Climate
York has a temperate maritime climate, with mild temperatures throughout the year. However, the weather can be unpredictable, and it is advisable to check the forecast before your trip. Summers are generally warm, with temperatures averaging around 20°C (68°F), while winters are cool, with temperatures ranging from 0°C to 10°C (32°F to 50°F). Rainfall is spread throughout the year, with the wettest months being November and December.

13.9 Language Tips and Useful Phrases
English is the main language spoken in York, and most locals will speak it fluently. However, if you want to impress the locals, here are a few useful phrases in the Yorkshire dialect:
- "Ey up": A greeting that means "hello" or "hi"
- "Ta": Short for "thank you"
- "Nowt": Means "nothing"
- "Ginnel": A narrow alleyway
- "Chuffin'ell": An expression of surprise or disbelief

13.10 Safety Tips for Solo and Female Travelers
York is generally a safe city for solo and female travelers. However, it is always advisable to take basic precautions to ensure your safety, such as:
- Stay in well-lit areas and avoid walking alone at night
- Keep your valuables secure and be aware of pickpocketing in crowded areas

- Trust your instincts and don't be afraid to say no or walk away from uncomfortable situations
- Research and plan your route in advance to avoid getting lost
- Use licensed taxis or rideshare services, especially at night.

Family-Friendly York

14.1 Kid-Friendly Attractions

York has a variety of family-friendly attractions that kids will love, including:

- JORVIK Viking Centre: An interactive museum that brings the Viking era to life, complete with reconstructed Viking streets and authentic smells.
- National Railway Museum: A museum dedicated to the history of the railway in Britain, with exhibits ranging from steam engines to modern trains.
- York Dungeon: A spooky attraction that takes visitors on a tour of York's dark past, with live actors, special effects, and interactive exhibits.
- York's Chocolate Story: A museum dedicated to the history of chocolate in York, with interactive exhibits and a chance to create your own chocolate treats.

14.2 Family Dining Options

York offers plenty of family-friendly dining options, including:

- Bettys Café Tea Rooms: A local institution known for its traditional afternoon tea and delicious cakes.
- York Roast Co.: Famous for its roast sandwiches, this casual eatery offers a range of delicious meat and vegetarian options.
- Pizza Express: A popular chain restaurant that offers delicious pizza and pasta dishes, as well as a dedicated children's menu.
- Wagamama: A family-friendly chain that serves up tasty Asian-inspired dishes, including noodles, curries, and bao buns.

14.3 Outdoor Activities and Parks

York has plenty of outdoor spaces for families to enjoy, including:

- Rowntree Park: A beautiful park that offers playgrounds, sports fields, and a lake for boating and fishing.
- York Maze: A giant maze that is open during the summer months and offers a range of family-friendly activities, including mini golf, go-karts, and a giant inflatable pillow.
- York City Walls: A walk along the city walls offers stunning views of the city and a chance to learn about York's history.
- York Minster Gardens: The gardens surrounding York Minster offer a peaceful retreat from the busy city, with beautiful flower beds and a small playground for children.

14.4 Child-Friendly Accommodation

Many of York's hotels and guesthouses offer family-friendly accommodation options, including:

- Premier Inn: A popular chain hotel that offers spacious family rooms and a child-friendly breakfast menu.
- Novotel York Centre: A family-friendly hotel that offers a range of amenities for children, including a play area and kids' meals.
- The Grand York: A luxury hotel that offers family rooms and a range of family-friendly amenities, including board games and coloring books.

14.5 Tips for Traveling with Children

When traveling with children, it's important to plan ahead and be prepared. Here are some tips for a stress-free family trip to York:

- Pack plenty of snacks and drinks to keep children fed and hydrated throughout the day.
- Bring a stroller or carrier for young children, as the city can be tiring to walk around.
- Plan ahead and book tickets for popular attractions and events to avoid long queues.
- Bring games, books, and other forms of entertainment to keep children occupied during travel and downtime.
- Research family-friendly restaurants and dining options ahead of time to avoid stress and hunger.

Beyond York: Exploring Yorkshire

16.1 Historic Cities and Towns

York is just one of many historic cities and towns in Yorkshire. Consider exploring other destinations with fascinating stories to tell and charming architecture to admire, such as:

- Harrogate: A spa town with beautiful gardens and a Victorian-era atmosphere.
- Ripon: A small market town with a stunning cathedral and a rich history dating back to the 7th century.
- Beverley: A picturesque town with a magnificent Gothic church and cobbled streets lined with independent shops and cafes.
- Whitby: A coastal town with a dramatic clifftop abbey, a historic harbour, and connections to Bram Stoker's Dracula.

16.2 Coastal Towns and Beaches

Yorkshire has a long coastline with plenty of charming seaside towns and beaches to explore. Some of the most popular destinations include:

- Scarborough: A bustling seaside resort with sandy beaches, amusement parks, and a historic castle.
- Filey: A peaceful seaside town with a long stretch of golden sand and rugged cliffs to explore.
- Robin Hood's Bay: A picturesque fishing village with narrow streets and alleys leading down to a pebble beach.
- Staithes: A quaint fishing village with a small harbour and colourful cottages lining the steep cliffs.

16.3 Scenic Drives and Outdoor Adventures

Yorkshire's natural beauty is best explored on foot or by car. Here are some of the best scenic drives and outdoor adventures to embark on:

- Yorkshire Dales Scenic Drive: A picturesque drive through the Yorkshire Dales National Park, featuring stunning vistas of rolling hills, waterfalls, and quaint villages.
- Yorkshire Three Peaks Challenge: A demanding but rewarding hike that takes you to the summit of three of the highest peaks in Yorkshire: Pen-y-ghent, Whernside, and Ingleborough.

- Humber Bridge Walk: A pedestrian path along one of the longest suspension bridges in the world, offering panoramic views of the Humber estuary and surrounding countryside.
- Yorkshire Coastline Drive: A scenic drive along the coast, passing through charming towns and villages like Whitby, Robin Hood's Bay, and Filey.

Three-Day Detailed York Itinerary

Day 1

Arrive Bootham Bar: 10:00

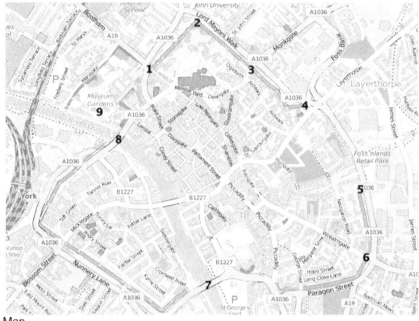

Map
1: City Walls Walk

Whether you're arriving in York today or stayed here overnight, start your exploring on Day 1 early so that you can get the best views of the city from the city walls.

Walk the City Walls: 10:00 — 12:00
See Map 1.
FREE. If the weather is good, the best way to take in York upon arrival is a walk around the city walls. Allow two hours for the entire circular route.

Starting from the **Bootham Bar (1)**, on the site of a Roman gate, head clockwise (north-east) to **Robin Hood Tower (2),** and continue to **Monk Bar (3),** which is the best preserved medieval gate and still has a working portcullis. This is the section of wall with the best views, especially of York Minster. Continue round to **Lathorpe Tower (4),** where you'll need to walk along Foss Islands Road until you reach **Red Tower (5)**, where you'll rejoin the walls. Continue to **Walmgate Bar (6),** England's only gate with an intact barbican, and continue until you hit the road again. You'll need to cross **Skeldergate Bridge (7)** before rejoining the walls for your final stretch, round the south-west side of the city until you reach **Lendal Bridge (8)** over the River Ouse. Cross the bridge and turn left into the **Museum Gardens (9)**.

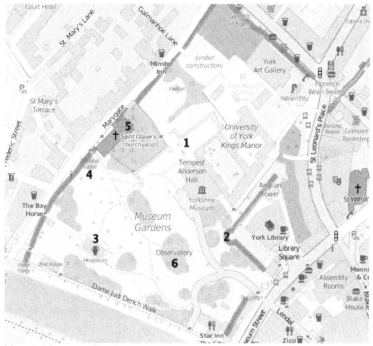

Map 2: Museum Gardens

Explore the Museum Gardens: 12:00 — 13:00

See Map 2

FREE. Your trip around the city walls will drop you off just outside the grounds of the peaceful Museum Gardens, which are well worth a visit. The Gardens are on the former grounds of **St Mary's Abbey (1)**, which you can still see the ruins of, and so the gardens contain many historic buildings within. Check out the **Multangular Tower (2)**, the **Hospitium (3)**, **St Mary's Lodge (4)**, **St Olave's Church (5)** and the **Observatory (6)**. There are information screens dotted around the Gardens which can provide you with historical context.

Lunch at Betty's: 13:00 — 14:30
See Map 3

No trip to Yorkshire would be complete without a trip to Betty's (1), the undisputed home of Afternoon Tea. With locations in upper-class York, Harrogate and Ilkley, Betty's is the epitome of posh. You'll be served by waiters in white aprons and the collection of teapots along the walls will amaze you, as well the range of cutlery and crockery you'll be dining on. Main courses range from £6-14, while Afternoon Tea will cost £18.50. Pricey, but well worth the experience.

York Architectural Marvels: 14:30 — 18:00
See Map 3

It's time to get stuck in to the heart of the city. Once you're full of scones, jam and butter, head past St Helen's Stonegate (2) and down Stonegate towards the marvel that is York Minster (3), £10/FREE. The Minster is York's cathedral and is built in the Gothic style, with a stunning wide nave and some staggering stained-glass windows. You can pay an extra £5 if you want to climb the tower — this is highly recommended for superb views of the city, if you can manage the 275 steps! With that ticket, you'll get to see the Undercroft, Treasury and Crypt, all located beneath the church, which are architecturally outstanding and contain some amazingly ancient relics. Once you're done in the Minster, head either across Dean's Park or along the Queen's Path towards the Treasurer's House (4), £7/£3.50. Good-looking on the outside, this used to be the home of York Minster's medieval treasurers, and the inside contains some fine furniture and gives you a great insight into 18th century life in Britain. Head down Goodramgate to the Holy Trinity Church (5), FREE, which has survived almost unchanged for almost 200 years and rests within a gloriously peaceful atmosphere. If you have time, head to the York Art Gallery, FREE, before it shuts at 5pm for some art browsing.

Day 2

The Shambles: 09:00 — 10:00
See Map 4

FREE. Your second day in York is a packed one, so it's best to start early by arriving at **The Shambles (1)** from wherever your accommodation is around 9am, and bring some lunch with you! The Shambles is an amazing medieval street with overhanging timber-framed buildings which was once the home of numerous butchers. The name of the street, in fact, comes from the hooks on which they used to display their meat, which are still visible outside the buildings today.

Dig: 10:00 — 12:00
See Map 4

£6/£5.50. Before today's highlight, it's worth popping in to Dig (2), which gives you the chance to try being an archeologist and unearth some of York's distant past, as well as learning about the archeological trade in the process. The guides can vary, and it's tailored mainly towards children, but it's hands on and very entertaining if you're keen on that kind of thing.

The Blue Bell: 12:00 — 12:30
See Map 4

The perfect place for a quick beer or other refreshment, **The Blue Bell (3)** is a prime example of a real English pub: the room is tiny, wood panelled and has a cosy fireplace, but its size and popularity often mean it's very full. Recommendations while you're there are the local brews, Timothy Taylor or Black Sheep, and a quick board game in the corner while eavesdropping on the many and varied conversations around you.

Jorvik Viking Centre: 12:30 — 15:00
See Map 4

£9.95/£6.95. Easily the best museum in town, the Jorvik Viking Centre (4) uses a self-styled 'time warp' experience to fully immerse visitors in what life would have been like in Viking England. It's a complete reconstruction of the Viking settlement unearthed in York in the 70s, and it will give you a fantastic insight into the 9th century way of life.

Tip: You can book your tickets and time slot online for an extra £1 to avoid queueing.

Clifford's Tower: 15:00 — 16:00
See Map 4

£4.30/£2.60. Mainly used these days for some good views over the city, Clifford's Tower **(5)** is what remains of York Castle. There's not much to see inside, but if the weather is fine, the views over the city, and over the **Eye of York (6)** can be quite evocative.

Museum Time: 16:00 — 17:00
See Map 4

Depending on your tastes, you have time to visit one more museum before they shut for the day. Options are Fairfax House **(7)**, **£6/FREE,** an old Georgian townhouse that's arguably prettier on the outside, or York Castle Museum **(8), £10/FREE,** which houses an exceptional collection of social history and boasts a gorgeous exterior. We recommend checking out the exterior of Fairfax House before a quick look around York Castle Museum before moving on.

Sunset River Walk: 17:00 — 18:00
See Map 4

FREE. The River Ouse is lovely at night, and you can start your walk from the **Tower Gardens (9)** and head towards the Ouse Bridge (north-west) where the best views of the riverside architecture can be found, especially if the light is right. Enjoy a stroll before grabbing some well-deserved dinner in town after a long day.

Dinner Time: 18:00 — 20:00
See Map 3

Cafe Concerto **(7),** which has a great selection of Mediterranean food in the evenings, is the place to go for dinner tonight. It's hugely popular with tourists and locals alike, and with dinner-time prices around £13-18, it's not going to make a huge whole in your wallet. You'll be impressed at the quality of the food, the size of the portions, and the smooth jazz coming from the radio will give you the feels.

Dinner Time, Cocktails and Dancing: 18:00 — 01:00
See Map 3

There are several options for dinner in this part of town. We recommend **1331 (8)** tonight, because it's an all-in-one affair: it's a courtyard complex with a bar, cocktail lounge and even a private cinema. You could spend all night here! Head to the first-floor restaurant which serves all the British classics like Bangers & Mash, Lamb Shank and Steak & Chips, before popping back downstairs to kick-start the night with some cocktails or a pint if you're that way inclined. The whole courtyard is open until 1am tonight, and is one of the most popular spots in town, so you'll easily make plenty of new friends and dance the night away. Expect to pay around **£9-17** for a main course.

Day 2 Map

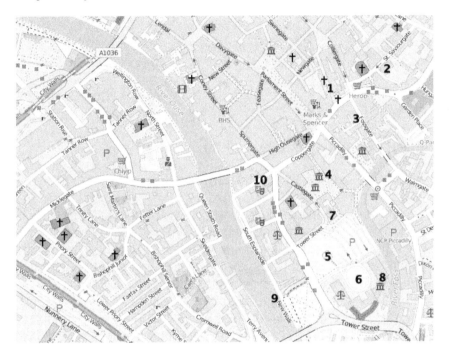

Map 4: South Central York

Grand Opera House: 20:00 — 22:00
See Map 4

The <u>Grand Opera House</u> (10) is the ideal place to spend a cultured Saturday evening. Contrary to the name, doesn't provide operatic performances but popular musicals, pantomimes, and comedy. Check the website by clicking the name above to see what's on offer tonight. Tickets are available online and on the door.

61

Day 3
Map 5: York Railway Station + National Railway Museum

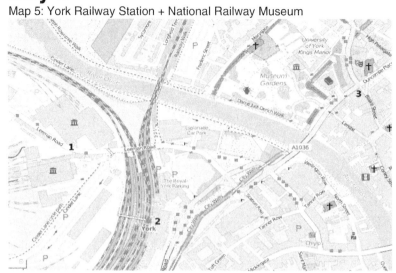

Castle Howard: 08:00 — 16:00
See Map 5

House & Grounds £14/£7.50, Grounds only £9.50/£6. For your final day in and around York, head to <u>Castle Howard</u>. Castle Howard isn't in York, but the most convenient way of getting there is via a York tour agency or by bus from York. At the **Tourist Information Office (3)** there are up-to-date schedules of all tour departures to Castle Howard, while <u>Stephenson's of Easingwold</u> offer a bus service for £7.50 return three times a day. Castle Howard is a breathtaking stately home, one of the most ornate in Britain, and was the scene for the film Brideshead Revisited. Allow almost a full day to appreciate everything the place has to offer. You'll be able to grab lunch there too, or take a packed lunch with you.

National Railway Museum: 16:00 — 18:00
See Map 5

FREE. The last leg on your tour of York (and an especially convenient and fitting one if you're heading out of town via train), is the <u>National Railway Museum</u> **(1).** I know what you're thinking - this place is for geeks and trainspotters! Wrong. This is the biggest Railway Museum in the world and is crammed full of things that would interest even the ordinary folk among us. Two hours is about right for your Average Joe to appreciate what the exhibits have to offer, before you head to the **Railway Station (2).**

Two-Day York Itinerary

Day 1:

- 9:00 AM: Begin the day by visiting York Minster, one of the most iconic landmarks in the city. The Gothic cathedral boasts impressive stained glass windows, intricate carvings, and a stunning central tower. Take your time exploring the interior and admiring the architecture.
- 11:00 AM: After leaving the Minster, take a stroll through the historic Shambles area. This charming medieval street is lined with timber-framed buildings and features unique shops, cafes, and street performers.
- 12:30 PM: Stop for lunch at one of the many local pubs, such as The Golden Fleece or The Duke of York. Enjoy some traditional pub fare like fish and chips or a hearty pie.
- 2:00 PM: In the afternoon, explore the city walls. York's walls are the longest and best-preserved medieval walls in England, and offer stunning views of the city. Stop at York Castle Museum, which tells the story of everyday life in the city from the Victorian era to the present day. Then, climb up to Clifford's Tower for panoramic views of the city.
- 4:00 PM: Take a break and grab a coffee or tea at one of the many cozy cafes in the city center.
- 5:00 PM: Spend some time shopping for souvenirs and local crafts in the independent shops and boutiques scattered throughout the city center.
- 7:00 PM: End the day with dinner at one of the city's top restaurants. Roots York is a Michelin-starred restaurant that offers a modern take on traditional British cuisine, while The Ivy St. Helen's Square features an elegant setting and a menu of international dishes.

Day 2:

- 9:00 AM: Begin the day at the JORVIK Viking Centre, an interactive museum that brings York's Viking history to life. Take a ride on a reconstructed Viking street and see artifacts from the Viking era.

- 11:00 AM: Next, head to the York Museum Gardens, which feature the remains of St. Mary's Abbey and a beautiful botanical garden. Take a stroll through the gardens and enjoy the peaceful surroundings.
- 12:30 PM: For lunch, head to the Shambles Market, which offers a variety of street food options from around the world. Try some local specialties like Yorkshire pudding or a pork pie.
- 2:00 PM: In the afternoon, visit the Treasurer's House, a hidden gem in the heart of the city. This historic house boasts beautiful gardens and impressive architecture. Take a guided tour to learn more about its fascinating history.
- 4:00 PM: Take a relaxing walk along the River Ouse, which winds through the city center. Stop at one of the riverside pubs, such as The Lowther, for a pint and some pub snacks.
- 6:00 PM: If you're interested in live theater, catch a performance at one of the city's many venues, such as the York Theatre Royal or the Grand Opera House.
- 8:00 PM: End the day with a nightcap at one of the city's cozy pubs, such as The Blue Bell or The Golden Lion.

Four & Five-Day York and Yorkshire Coast Itinerary

Day 1:
9:00 AM - Begin your day with a visit to York Minster, one of the most iconic landmarks in the city. Explore the stunning cathedral and learn about its rich history and architecture.

11:00 AM - Head over to the historic Shambles area, a narrow street lined with timber-framed buildings dating back to the 14th century. Take a stroll through the quaint alleyways and browse the unique shops and cafes.

1:00 PM - Enjoy lunch at one of York's local pubs, such as The Golden Fleece or The Duke of York. Both offer traditional British fare and a cozy atmosphere.

2:30 PM - Take a trip to the nearby York Designer Outlet for some shopping. With over 100 designer and high street brands, you're sure to find some great deals.

6:00 PM - End the day with dinner at one of York's excellent restaurants, such as The Whippet Inn or Skosh. Both offer modern twists on traditional British cuisine.

Day 2:

9:00 AM - Take a day trip to the historic coastal town of Whitby. Start with a visit to the stunning Whitby Abbey, which inspired Bram Stoker's Dracula. Learn about the history of the abbey and enjoy the stunning views over the town and coast.

11:00 AM - Stroll through the charming town center and explore the unique shops and galleries. Don't forget to stop at the famous Whitby Jet shops, which sell the town's signature black gemstone.

1:00 PM - Enjoy lunch at one of the local seafood restaurants, such as The Magpie Cafe or Trenchers. Both offer fresh seafood and stunning views over the harbor.

3:00 PM - Take a relaxing walk along the beach and visit some of the town's other attractions, such as the Captain Cook Memorial Museum or the Dracula Experience.

6:00 PM - Return to York and enjoy dinner at one of the city's top restaurants, such as Roots York or The Ivy St. Helen's Square.

Day 3:

9:00 AM - Spend the morning at the JORVIK Viking Centre, a fascinating museum that tells the story of York's Viking history. Explore the interactive exhibits and learn about life in a Viking settlement.

11:00 AM - Head over to the York Museum Gardens, which features the remains of St. Mary's Abbey and stunning botanical gardens. Take a stroll through the gardens and enjoy the peaceful atmosphere.

1:00 PM - Enjoy lunch at the Shambles Market, which offers a variety of local street food and artisanal products.

2:30 PM - Take a stroll along the River Ouse and visit the Clifford's Tower, a medieval castle keep that offers stunning views over the city.

7:00 PM - In the evening, enjoy a ghost walk or haunted experience, such as the Original Ghost Walk of York or York Dungeon. Learn about York's spooky history and legends.

Day 4:

9:00 AM - Start the day with a visit to the Treasurer's House, a hidden gem in the heart of the city. Explore the stunning 17th-century mansion and its beautiful gardens.

11:00 AM - Head over to the nearby York Castle Museum, which tells the story of York's history through interactive exhibits and displays. Learn about life in the city during different time periods.

1:00 PM - Enjoy lunch at one of York's local cafes, such as Mannion & Co or The Hairy Fig. Both offer delicious homemade food and a cozy atmosphere.

2:30 PM - Explore the city walls and visit the impressive York Art Gallery, which houses a collection of British art from the 14th century to the present day.

7:00 PM - End the day with dinner at one of York's top restaurants, such as Skosh or The Whippet Inn. Both offer modern twists on traditional British cuisine and a sophisticated atmosphere.

Day 5:

9:00 AM - Take a day trip to the stunning North York Moors National Park, a vast expanse of heather-covered moorland, forests, and valleys. Start your visit with a trip to the charming village of Hutton-le-Hole, which features traditional thatched-roof cottages and a fascinating museum.

11:00 AM - Visit the North Yorkshire Moors Railway, a heritage railway that takes you on a scenic journey through the park. Enjoy stunning views over the moors and forests as you ride on a vintage steam train.

1:00 PM - Enjoy lunch at one of the local pubs or cafes in the area, such as The Horseshoe Inn or The Moors Inn. Both offer traditional British fare and a cozy atmosphere.

3:00 PM - Take a walk through the picturesque town of Pickering, which features a castle and a variety of shops and cafes.

7:00 PM - Return to York and end your trip with a farewell dinner at one of the city's top restaurants, such as Roots York or The Ivy St. Helen's Square.

Thank You!

With its rich history, stunning architecture, and charming streets, York is a must-visit destination for any traveler. Whether you're interested in exploring the city's famous landmarks, immersing yourself in its culture and cuisine, or venturing out to the nearby countryside and coast, there is something for everyone in York. We hope this travel guide and all our itineraries have given you some inspiration for your trip and helped you plan an unforgettable experience in this beautiful part of the UK.

Printed in Great Britain
by Amazon

41546689R00040